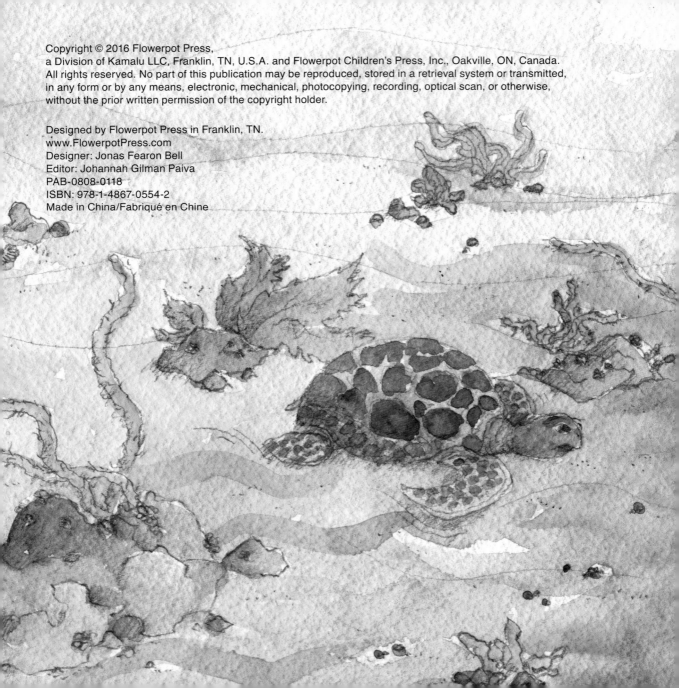

Designed by Flowerpot Press in Franklin, TN.
www.FlowerpotPress.com
Designer: Jonas Fearon Bell
Editor: Johannah Gilman Paiva
PAB-0808-0118
ISBN: 978-1-4867-0554-2
Made in China/Fabriqué en Chine

Why Do Sea Turtles

Jennifer Shand

Illustrated by
T. G. Tjornehoj

Look Like
They are Crying?

How do animals survive in the ocean? The ocean is very large and has many predators. Each animal must have something special about them to live there.

Why do BLUE WHALES not have TEETH?

Is it because they DON'T LIKE going
to the DENTIST?

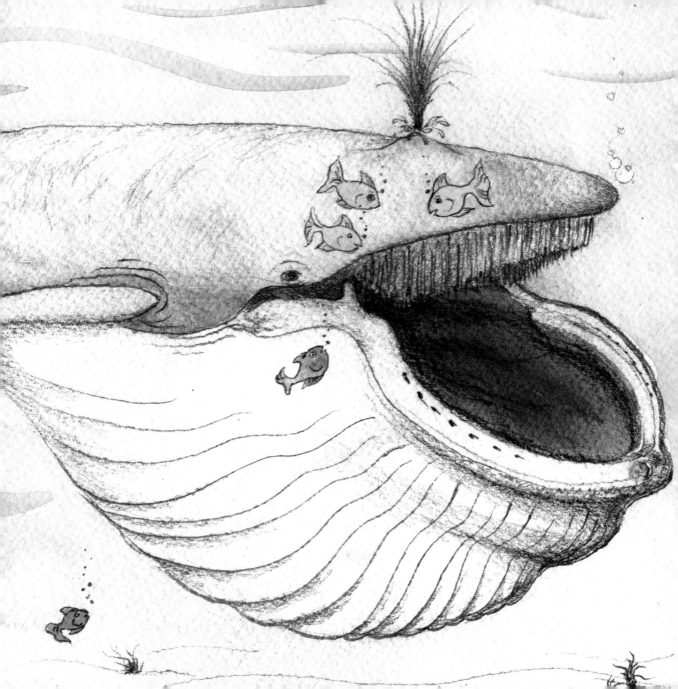

No, that's silly!

Blue whales belong to a group called "baleen whales" that have bristles instead of teeth. When a blue whale opens its mouth and ocean water comes in, the bristles act like a strainer, keeping the food in, while letting the water back out. They also do not need teeth because they swallow their food whole!

Why do sea TURTLES sometimes look like they are CRYING?

Is it because they have a BOO-BOO?

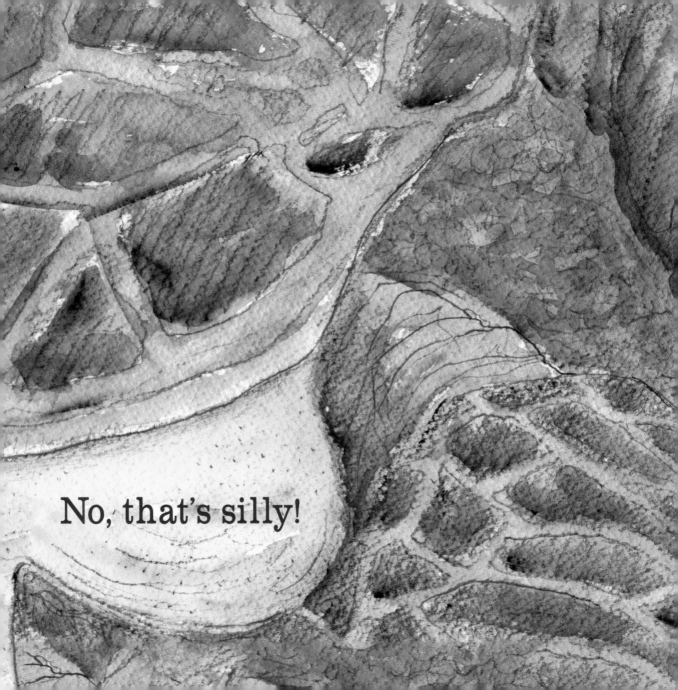

No, that's silly!

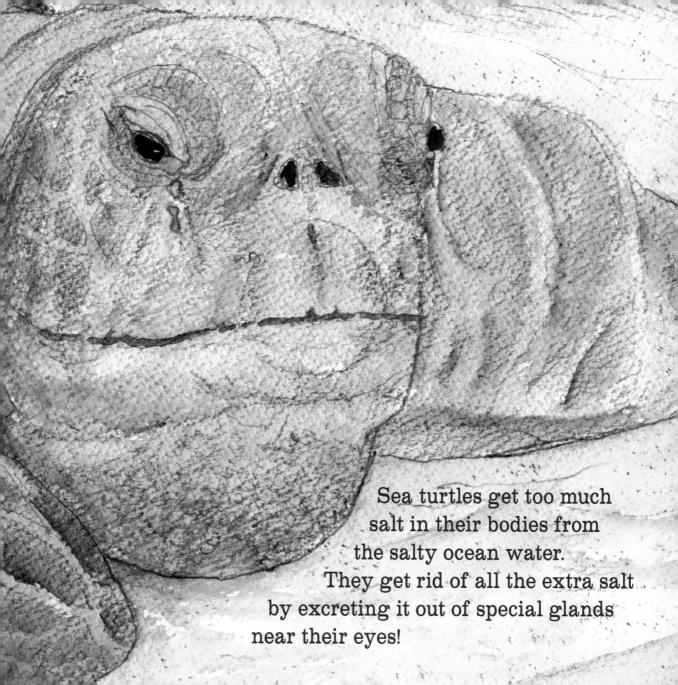

Sea turtles get too much
salt in their bodies from
the salty ocean water.
They get rid of all the extra salt
by excreting it out of special glands
near their eyes!

Why do STARFISH have STICKY feet?

Is it because they spilled MAPLE SYRUP
all over the PLACE?

No, that's silly!

Starfish have naturally sticky feet that allow them to walk along the ocean floor and grip it even though they are under water! It also helps them hold their food while in the water!

Why do FISH not have EYELIDS?

Is it because they are AFRAID of the DARK?

Fish do not have
eyelids because
they do not need
them. Eyelids are for
keeping eyes moist,
and since fish are in
the water, their eyes
do not get dry!

Why do WALRUSES have so much
FAT on their bodies?

Is it because they EAT too many
DOUGHNUTS?

The Original
DOUGHNUT
DOME

Please take
a number

No, that's silly!

Walruses live and swim in the coldest waters of the ocean, so they have a thick layer of fat under their skin called "blubber" that keeps them warm!

The animals in the ocean sometimes do funny things or have funny features, but it is all so they can survive there. It is a good thing, because if animals could not live in the ocean, there would be so many fewer animals on Earth, and these animals are vital for the survival of many creatures, including humans. The animals in the ocean are a very important part of life for all of us!